TEDDY BEAR TALES

A collection of twelve favourite teddy bear stories.

FOREWORD BY SUSANNA GRETZ

A Red Fox Book

Published by Random House Children's Books
20 Vauxhall Bridge Road, London SW1V 2SA

A division of The Random House Group Ltd
London Melbourne Sydney Auckland
Johannesburg and agencies throughout the world

This edition © copyright Hutchinson Children's Books 1997
Text and illustrations © copyright individual authors and illustrators; see below

1 3 5 7 9 10 8 6 4 2

First published in Great Britain by
Hutchinson Children's Books 1997
Red Fox 2000

This book is sold subject to the condition that it shall not, by way of trade
or otherwise, be lent, resold, hired out, or otherwise circulated without the
publisher's prior consent in any form of binding or cover other than that in
which it is published and without a similar condition including this
condition being imposed on the subsequent purchaser.

The authors and illustrators have asserted their right under
the Copyright, Designs and Patents Act, 1988, to be identified
as the authors and illustrators of this work

Printed in Hong Kong by Midas Printing Ltd.

THE RANDOM HOUSE GROUP Limited Reg. No. 954009
www.randomhouse.co.uk

ISBN 0 09 940913 5

ACKNOWLEDGEMENTS
Foreword © Susanna Gretz 1997

Little Bear Lost text and illustrations © Jane Hissey 1989; *Jenny's Bear* text © Michael Ratnett 1991, illustrations © June Goulding 1991; *Ruby* text and illustrations © Maggie Glen 1990; *The Wild Bears* and *Bad Mood Bear* text and illustrations © John Richardson 1989 and 1987; *Tiny Ted's Big Adventure* text and illustrations © Peter Bowman 1994; *Rosie and the Pavement Bears* text and illustrations © Susie Jenkin-Pearce 1991; *Grandpa Bodley and the Photographs* text © Caroline Castle 1993, illustrations © Peter Bowman 1993; *Something New for a Bear to Do* text © Shirley Isherwood 1993, illustrations © Reg Cartwright 1993; *Watch Out for Fred!* text and illustrations © Suzy-Jane Tanner 1991; all originally published by Hutchinson Children's Books; *Bear in the Air* text and illustrations © Benedict Blathwayt 1991; first published by Julia MacRae Books; *Teddybears on Stage* illustrations © Susanna Gretz 1990, text © Alison Sage 1990, first published by A & C Black

CONTENTS

FOREWORD BY SUSANNA GRETZ..... 4

LITTLE BEAR LOST *Jane Hissey* 6

JENNY'S BEAR *Michael Ratnett & June Goulding* 14

RUBY *Maggie Glen* 24

THE WILD BEARS *John Richardson* 34

TINY TED'S BIG ADVENTURE *Peter Bowman* 44

ROSIE AND THE PAVEMENT BEARS *Susie Jenkin-Pearce* 52

BEAR IN THE AIR *Benedict Blathwayt* 66

GRANDPA BODLEY AND THE PHOTOGRAPHS *Caroline Castle & Peter Bowman* 76

BAD MOOD BEAR *John Richardson* 86

SOMETHING NEW FOR A BEAR TO DO *Shirley Isherwood & Reg Cartwright* 96

TEDDYBEARS ON STAGE *Susanna Gretz & Alison Sage* 108

WATCH OUT FOR FRED! *Suzy-Jane Tanner* 118

FOREWORD

I HAVE just had a close look at all the teddy bears in this Treasury. How different everyone else's look! In fact, many people have assured me that my particular bears aren't really teddies, but children dressed in bear suits. Nevertheless, I can't help noticing that the other bears in this book don't all look alike either. In fact, they range from the more well-known toy-shop variety, as in *Tiny Ted's Big Adventure*, *Watch Out for Fred!* and *Bear in the Air*, to creatures somewhat more bear than teddy, as in *Rosie and the Pavement Bears* and *Something New for a Bear to Do*. *Jenny's Bears* includes some of each sort. Without doubt, they are all chubby, furry, cuddly and endearing; yet I sense there's more to them than this.

In reading the stories collected here, I was struck by just how much teddy bears can do! Children learn very early on that these characters are "on their side". This gives stories about teddy bears a head start. They are so appealing that no one can help wanting to be their friend – and they usually look as if they want to be ours. Straight away, they manage to make a firm bond with their audience. When, for instance, Grandpa Bodley sheds a few tears over the family photos, I am willing to bet that young children have a sense of how he must feel. Is it partly because he's a bear? I suspect it is.

At the same time, teddy bears can behave like grown-ups without risking their necks – just because they're teddy bears. They generally avoid crossing over into the roles usually filled by parents and other carers. In *Little Bear Lost*, Old Bear has the foresight to prepare a picnic for the other toys, and the sensitivity to comfort Rabbit after his mistake with the slipper. He has adult tact and common sense, but he loves to play hide-and-seek, too. And Ruby, Maggie Glen's "special bear", also plays at least two roles: a small child being bullied and a very grown-up revolutionary.

In *The Wild Bears*, John Richardson's characters may let young audiences see themselves as both "tame" and "wild" more easily than they might if those characters were real children. Sara, as the impatient manager in *Teddybears on Stage*, may just get more sympathy – for the same reason. And while, in *Something New for a Bear to Do*, Edward James and Mr Manders might appear unrealistic if they were people, as bears they are able to exchange roles long enough to explore the exciting notion that adults (not only children!) can have silly ideas, and may need help in recognising their own talents.

So it seems to me that teddy bears permit their authors very special liberties. Alas, adults aren't always comfortable with these liberties. They have sometimes asked me, How can your bears move house, drive to the seaside, put on a play, etc., with hardly an adult in sight, bar the occasional waiter, ticket collector, or uncle who lives a train journey away? It's because they're teddy bears, I try to explain. Children, in contrast, find it completely acceptable that teddies do all these things as well as play children's games, wreak havoc in the supermarket and so on.

Probably it's because they don't have to act either completely like adults or completely like children that teddy bears are so good at clothing instruction and insight with lots of comfort, reassurance and good humour. As these stories surely prove, they are quite a phenomenon. And no matter how much we think teddy bears can do, there will always be room for them to do more!

SUSANNA GRETZ

Jane Hissey
LITTLE BEAR LOST

OLD BEAR HAD BEEN BUSY ALL MORNING. He'd packed an enormous picnic for all the toys. There were sandwiches, cakes, buns, pies and jellies.

"I think I've put in a bit too much food," he said to himself as he sat on the picnic-basket lid to try to make it close.

Suddenly in a blur of fur and red trousers, Little Bear dashed past the basket and dived into a heap of books. "Do you think anyone will find me?" he asked from the middle of the heap.

"I shouldn't think so," said Old Bear. "Who's looking for you?"

But before Little Bear could answer, the door flew open and into the room ran Bramwell Brown, Duck and Rabbit. They didn't seem to be looking for Little Bear and, in a moment, they were hiding too. Rabbit and Duck were behind the curtains and Bramwell's feet could just be seen sticking out from under a cushion.

"We're playing hide-and-seek," explained the cushion in a Bramwell Brown sort of voice. "Did anyone see us hide?"

"Only me," said Old Bear, "but who's looking for you?"

There was a bit of a silence and then the cushion moved.

Little Bear Lost • Jane Hissey

Bramwell looked sadly up at Old Bear. "Oh dear," he said, miserably, "we've done it again. We've forgotten to have a seeker in our game of hide-and-seek."

The others crept out of their hiding places and sat down on Bramwell's cushion.

"What a pity," said Duck. "It could have been a good game, too."

"Old Bear," said Little Bear, thoughtfully, "if we all hide again, could you look for us?"

Old Bear said that was a good idea and, with paws over his eyes, he slowly counted to ten. "One, two, three," he began, as Rabbit jumped into a vase and tried to look like a bunch of flowers.

"Four, five, six," he continued, as Duck jumped into a shoe box.

"Seven, eight, nine," he said, giving Bramwell time to hide a last bit of paw.

"TEN," he called, "I'm READY!" And by then Little Bear had also disappeared.

Old Bear looked all around the room to see whether any paws or ears were showing. It wasn't very tidy.

First he found a sock that he'd lost weeks ago. And then he found at least ten marbles that had rolled underneath things. He even found Cat, who wasn't really lost or hiding, and Cat helped him look for the others. But he couldn't find them.

"It's no good," he sighed. "I can't find any of you. I can only find things I'm *not* looking for. Can we tidy up a bit and then start again?"

One by one the other toys wriggled out of their secret hiding places. All of them, that is, except Little Bear.

"Where's Little Bear?" asked Bramwell Brown, but nobody seemed to know.

"Well, he can't be far away," said Old Bear. "Let's give him a shout."

They all climbed up on a chair and called "LITTLE BEAR" so loudly that they made themselves jump and almost fell off. Duck prodded all the cushions with his beak to see whether Little Bear was underneath, and Bramwell peered under the bed.

"He could be under here," he said.

"Well, I'm not going to look," said Duck. "It's dark and dusty."

"Oh, I'll go," said Rabbit. "It's just like a tunnel and I love tunnels." He was just about to dive under the bed when Bramwell grabbed him by the tail.

"Wait a minute, Rabbit," he said. "I'll give you the end of this string and then you won't get lost because we'll all be on the other end."

With the string tied round his middle, Rabbit bounded into the darkness. The others waited and watched.

Suddenly the string gave such a jerk that Duck fell on his beak.

"He's here, he's here!" squeaked Rabbit. "I'm holding on to him, can you pull us out?"

All together they pulled hard on the string and out popped Rabbit, tail first, clutching not Little Bear but...a fluffy slipper!

"Oh," said Duck, looking down at the slipper, "I don't think that's Little Bear."

"Of course it's not," said Bramwell. "He never looked like that."

"It *felt* like Little Bear," said Rabbit.

"It's not your fault, Rabbit," said Old Bear, kindly. "You were very brave to go in there on your own and I'm sure Little Bear will turn up soon."

"I bet he won't," said Duck, still gazing at the slipper. "He's probably wandered off and is miles away by now."

"Rubbish!" said Bramwell. "I expect he's just stuck in something. We must keep looking."

"I think we should make a poster saying 'This bear is lost', with a picture of Little Bear on it," said Old Bear. "Then all the toys will know who we're looking for."

The animals all fetched the painting things and Bramwell sat and painted a picture of a small bear in red trousers that did look quite a bit like Little Bear. There wasn't really enough room to write "This bear is lost", so they just made him look a bit sad and hoped that everyone would know what it meant.

Just to make sure, Bramwell called all the other toys together and explained what had happened. They all wanted to help and, within minutes, everyone was searching.

They rolled up rugs and climbed up curtains. They jumped into drawers and turned out toys. They peered behind plants and rummaged through rubbish.

They felt as though they'd searched through the whole house but still there

Little Bear Lost • Jane Hissey

was no sign of Little Bear.

"Phew, I'm tired," said Bramwell Brown.

"And I'm hungry," said Duck.

"Well," said Old Bear, "everyone has worked very hard and I think we all deserve our picnic. When we've eaten we'll start looking again."

He led the way to the picnic basket that he'd packed in the morning and lifted the lid.

"There," he said proudly. "What do you think of that?"

The animals all peered inside. But what they saw was not what they had expected to see.

There, lying tucked up under a tea cloth, fast asleep and looking very full, was Little Bear.

"Well, well!" gasped Bramwell Brown.

"Hmm, we seem to have found a bear and lost a picnic," said Duck, staring at the crumbs that covered Little Bear.

"It's a good thing I made too much then," said Old Bear. "There's still plenty left for us."

Bramwell Brown lifted Little Bear out of the basket and gave him a big hug.

"Come on, everyone," he called, "picnic time!"

Carefully, they dragged the basket bumpety bump down the stairs and out into the garden.

"This looks like a good place for a picnic," said Old Bear, spreading the cloth out under a tree.

They had a wonderful feast, finishing every crumb in the basket. Then they stretched out in the sun to rest.

"I know," said Little Bear, suddenly leaping to his feet, "let's have *another* game of hide-and-seek."

But there was no reply. Leaning against the tree and full of food, all the other toys were fast asleep.

Michael Ratnett
JENNY'S BEAR
Illustrated by June Goulding

Jenny had hundreds of bears of all shapes and sizes, and she loved every one of them. But what she wanted most in all the world was to meet a real live bear.

"Mum," she said one morning, "if we made a nice, cosy sort of den in the shed, would a real bear come and live in it?"

"I shouldn't think so," replied Mum kindly. "There aren't any real bears about here."

"Not even if I wished very hard?" said Jenny.

"I'm afraid not," said Mum. "But we can make a den just for you and your toy bears, if you like."

The shed was in a terrible state.

"Phew," said Mum, "I've never seen such a muddle. It must be years since this place was last cleaned!"

"It's no wonder that there aren't any bears living around here if all the sheds are this messy," said Jenny seriously.

"No wonder at all," said Mum.

When the den was ready, Jenny settled her bears in so that if a real bear did come he would feel at home among his own kind.

"There," she said. "You look just right. Now, I've got to go in for lunch, so you'll have to keep watch for me, and if a bear does turn up, be sure to make him welcome."

All through lunch Jenny kept wishing for a real bear to be waiting for her back in the den.

And then she hurried out to the shed with a tray full of special things for the bear to eat.

But the den was just as she had left it. There was no sign of a real bear anywhere.

"Bother!" said Jenny.

But she set out her tea things and her books just the same, and then sat down to wait patiently.

Jenny and her bears waited, and waited and waited. And just when it seemed that nobody was ever coming, there was a knock at the door.

16

"Come in," said Jenny.

And in stepped the biggest, brownest, friendliest-looking bear she had ever seen!

"Hello," he said. "I hope you don't mind me popping in, but I've come all the way from the Wild North searching for somewhere to spend the coming winter, and this is by far the cosiest-looking place I've found."

"Of course I don't mind," said Jenny. "I made this den specially for bears, and I've been wishing for a bear all day."

Then Jenny sat the bear down, and told him to help himself to the food. He had buns, biscuits and jelly, which he thought was wonderfully wobbly. But he was not at all sure about the tea Jenny poured out for him.

"Hmm," he said. "This cup doesn't look very full. What sort of tea is it?"

"It's *pretend* tea," said Jenny.

"Oh, that's all right then," said the bear. "Pretend tea is the sort that bears like best."

And he drank it all up in one go. "Another cup please,"

he said, "but not so much sugar this time thank you."

Then Jenny showed the bear her books.

"Which one would you like first?" she asked. "The happy one or the sad one?"

"The sad one," said the bear. "As long as it's not too sad."

But it was too sad.

"Boohoo, boohoo," blubbered the bear. "Stop it. You're making me cry!" And big tears ran down his furry face.

So Jenny read the funny story to cheer him up.

"Ho ho ho!" roared the bear. "No more, no more. My sides are going to split!" And they both rolled around on the floor until the whole shed shook.

"That was fun," said the bear. "What shall we do now?"

"I've got this," said Jenny, holding up a small bottle.

"Bubble mixture!" said the bear. "However did you guess? All bears love blowing bubbles."

Outside Jenny and the bear blew hundreds of shimmering bubbles.

"You're very good at this," said Jenny.

"My whole family are champion bubble-blowers," said the bear. "My grandad once blew a bubble that was so big it took him right up into the air, and carried him hundreds of miles away."

"Wow!" said Jenny. "Did he ever get home again?"

"Oh yes," said the bear. "He wrapped himself in brown paper and posted himself back. He was a very clever bear."

By the end of the day, Jenny and the bear were the closest of friends. So she was very sad when he said that it was time for him to go.

"But you said you were going to stay the winter," she said.

"Yes," said the bear. "It's not winter yet though, and I've got lots of things to do first."

"You will come back, won't you?" said Jenny. "And bring your friends."

"I'll try," said the bear. "But remember to keep wishing."

Then he gave Jenny a special bear hug, and set off down the road. Jenny waved the bear out of sight, and went indoors for supper.

The next morning Jenny jumped out of bed, dressed quickly, and ran out to the shed.

But the den was empty. The big brown bear who liked stories and blowing bubbles was not there.

"What's the matter?" said Mum.

"My bear's gone," said Jenny.

"Cheer up," said Mum, "you know there wasn't really a bear, don't you?"

The weeks went by, and the weather got colder; but though there was still no sign of the bear, Jenny never forgot him.

"There *was* a bear," she said to herself. "And he will come back. I just have to keep wishing."

Then it was Christmas morning. When Jenny drew back the curtains and looked out of the window, she saw something magical in the snowy garden.

She tugged on her coat and boots, and ran out for a better look.

"A Snowbear!" she gasped.

And then she saw the huge prints in the snow.

She followed them all the way to the shed.

Everything was silent as she carefully pushed open the door…

"SURPRISE!" roared a chorus of growly voices, for the shed was crowded with bears – real bears of every shape and size. And right in the middle sat Jenny's bear!

"I said I'd come back," he said. "And this time I've brought the tea,

and there's plenty for everyone."

"What kind of tea?" laughed Jenny.

"Why pretend, of course," said the bear.

"Oh, good,' said Jenny. "That's the kind I like best!"

Maggie Glen
RUBY

RUBY FELT DIFFERENT FROM OTHER BEARS – sort of special.

Mrs Harris had been day-dreaming when she made Ruby. She didn't notice that she'd used the spotted material that was meant for the toy leopards. She didn't watch carefully when she sewed on the nose.

Ruby wasn't surprised when she was chosen from the other bears, but she didn't like being picked up by her ear.

"OUCH, GET OFF!" she growled.

Ruby's paw was stamped with an "S" and she was thrown into the air.

"YIPEE-E-E-E! 'S' IS FOR SPECIAL," yelled Ruby.

Ruby flew across the factory and landed in a box full of bears.

"Hello," she said. "My name's Ruby and I'm special – see." She held up her paw.

"No silly," laughed a big bear. "'S' is for second – second best."

"We're mistakes," said the bear with rabbit ears. "When the box is full, we'll be thrown out."

Ruby's fur stood on end; she was horrified.

More bears joined them in the box. At last the machines stopped.

They listened to the workers as they chatted and hurried to catch the bus home. They heard the key turn in the lock. Then everything was quiet. One by one the bears fell asleep.

All except Ruby - Ruby was thinking. The only sound was the sound of the big bear snoring.

Hours passed. Suddenly Ruby shouted, "That's it!"

"What's it?" gasped the rabbit-eared bear who woke up with a fright.

"Zzzzzzzzzzzzzzzz-w-w-what's going on?" groaned the big bear, rubbing his sleepy eyes.

"That's *it*," said Ruby again. "We'll escape."

"ESCAPE!" they all shouted. And they jumped out of the box.

"Let's go!" said Ruby.

They looked for a way out.

They rattled the windows.

They pushed at the doors.

"There *is* no way out," cried a little bear. "We're trapped."

"This way," shouted Ruby, rushing into the cloakroom.

They found a broken air vent.

It was a very tight squeeze. They pushed and they pulled, they wriggled and they waggled, until they were all in the yard outside.

They ran silently, swiftly, through the night and into the day.

Some ran to the country, some to the town.

Some squeezed through letterboxes.

Some slipped through open windows.

Some hid in toy cupboards.

Some crept into bed with lonely children. But Ruby...

...climbed into the window of the very best toy shop in town.

The other toys stared at Ruby.

"What's the 'S' for?" squealed the pigs.

"Special," said Ruby, proudly.

All the toys shrieked with laughter.

"Scruffy," said the smart-looking penguin.

"Soppy," said the chimpanzee.

"Stupid," giggled the mice.

"Very strange for a bear," they all agreed.

"Don't come next to me," said a prim doll.

"Wouldn't want to," said Ruby.

"Stand at the back," shouted the other toys.

They poked, they pulled, they prodded and they pinched. Ruby pushed back as hard as she could, but there were too many of them.

So Ruby spent all day at the back of the shelf.

Then, just before closing time, a small girl came into the shop with her grandfather.

They searched and searched for something – something different, something special.

"That's the one," said the little girl.

"Yes, Susie," said Grandfather, "that one looks very special."

Ruby looked around her. "Can they see me? IT'S ME! They're pointing at me. WHOOPEE-E-E-E!"

"We'll have that one, please," said Grandfather.

The shopkeeper put Ruby on the counter.

She looked at the "S" on Ruby's paw.

"I'm sorry, sir," she said, "this one is a second. I'll fetch another."

"No thank you, that one is just perfect," said Grandfather. "It has character."

Character, thought Ruby, that sounds good.

"Shall I wrap it for you?" the shopkeeper asked.

"Not likely," growled Ruby. "Who wants to be shoved in a paper bag?"

"No thank you," said Susie. "I'll have her just as she is."

They all went out of the shop and down the street.

When they came to a yellow door they stopped.

"We're home, Spotty," said Susie.

"SPOTTY, WHAT A CHEEK!" muttered Ruby.

"It's got a growl," said Susie, and she and her grandfather laughed.

Susie took off her coat and scarf and sat Ruby on her lap.

Susie stared at Ruby and Ruby stared back.

Suddenly, Ruby saw a little silver "S" hanging on a chain round Susie's neck.

Hooray! thought Ruby. One of us – a special.

John Richardson
THE WILD BEARS

Before he set off for the day, young Jack Alabaster stood his two teddy bears by the door. "Keep guard while we are gone," he said sternly.

But he was being watched. Five wild teddy bears were hiding behind the potting shed; five naughty teddy bears looking for somewhere to live; five *hungry* teddy bears looking for something to eat.

There were Big Bear, Medium Bear, two small bears and a tiny little baby bear called Grub.

The Wild Bears • John Richardson

As soon as the family had gone, the five wild teddy bears marched straight up to the house and knock, knock, knocked on the big front door.

"You can't come in," said the two tame teddies.

But those five wild teddy bears marched right inside as bold as can be.

First they went into the kitchen.

"I spy honey!" cried Big Bear. They rubbed their teddy-bear tummies and licked their teddy-bear lips and rolled their teddy-bear eyes as Big Bear reached for the pot.

"You can't do that!" cried the two tame teddies.

"Don't worry," said Big Bear, "we won't make a mess."

But they did. And the little baby bear called Grub made the biggest mess of all.

Next, the five wild teddy bears marched upstairs and straight into Jack Alabaster's very own room.

"Toys!" cried Medium Bear.

"You can't play with those," screamed the two tame teddies.

"Don't worry," said Big Bear, "we won't break anything."

But they did…

The Wild Bears • John Richardson

Then those five wild teddy bears marched straight downstairs, through the hall, out the back door and into the garden.

"Oh, look at these lovely flowers!" cried the two small bears.

"You mustn't pick them," warned the two tame teddies.

"Don't worry," said Big Bear, "we won't pick many."

But they did. And the tiny little bear called Grub picked every one of Mr Alabaster's prize daisies and hung them round his neck.

"Oh, you naughty bears!" cried the two tame teddies in a fury. But the five wild teddy bears just marched round and round the garden, through the back door, down the hall and up the stairs.

The Wild Bears • John Richardson

"Bath time," said Big Bear and in a second the five wild teddies were all in the bath, rubbing and scrubbing and washing their fur and cleaning their ears and scrubbing their backs and splashing water *everywhere*. The two tame teddies had never seen such a mess.

When they were dry the five wild teddy bears made five hot-water bottles and carried them upstairs. Then they got straight into Jack Alabaster's very own bed and fell fast asleep.

"You can't sleep *here*!" cried the two tame teddies. But they could, and they did. And the tiny little baby bear called Grub slept the soundest of all.

But very soon there was a slamming noise and a clicking noise and an opening and a closing. Big Bear awoke with a start. "They're back!" he cried. And the wild teddies jumped out of bed and ran helter skelter down the stairs and through the hall and out the door and back behind the potting shed.

"Phew!" said Big Bear.

"Phew!" said Medium Bear.

"Phew!" said the two small bears together.

But the tiny little baby bear called Grub said nothing at all.

For he wasn't there!

From downstairs, Grub heard Mr Alabaster cry, "Just look at my garden. Who's been picking my flowers?"

"It wasn't us," said the two tame teddies. But nobody heard.

"And who's been eating the honey?" cried Sophie Alabaster from the kitchen.

"And who's been bathing in the bath and splashing water *everywhere*?" said Mrs Alabaster.

"Oh dear, oh dear, oh dear," sighed the two tame teddies.

And very, very close to Grub, Jack Alabaster cried, "Somebody's broken my space rocket!" Then he looked sternly at the two tame teddies. "I thought I asked you to keep guard," he said.

"It was those five wild teddies," said the two tame bears. But their teddy-bear voices were too small to be heard.

That night Jack woke up suddenly. There was a creaking noise, then, to his amazement, he saw the toy cupboard open and a small dark shape scamper across the room to the window and climb out.

He leapt out of bed just in time to see five small shadows at the bottom of the ivy. And, in the light of the moon, the five small shadows turned into five wild teddy bears.

"So *that's* who broke my space rocket!" gasped Jack.

"And picked the flowers and ate the honey and flooded the bathroom," said the two tame teddies. "And we *couldn't* make them stop."

As they watched from the window, the five wild bears ran across the lawn towards the forest.

"And don't come back!" shouted the two tame teddies.

"Don't worry, we won't," said the tiny little baby bear called Grub.

And they never did.

Peter Bowman
TINY TED'S BIG ADVENTURE

TINY TED woke up with a big yawn. "Breakfast time," said Mouse.

Tiny Ted's Big Adventure • Peter Bowman

"It's so quiet here," sighed Tiny Ted.

"I wonder what it's like out there."

"Phew, that was a tight squeeze…"

"…Oh, what a lovely morning. I think I'll have a little holiday."

"This is perfect!"

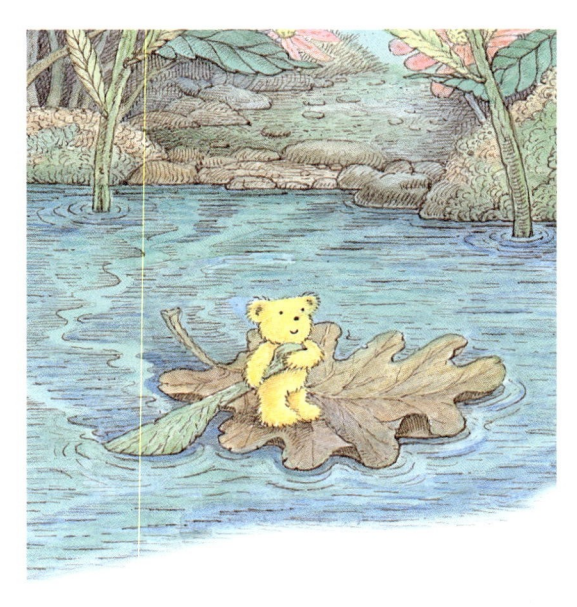

"I can go sailing..."    "...and sunbathing."

Tiny Ted's Big Adventure • Peter Bowman

"But, maybe there isn't room for two."

"Lucky I can swim. Whoa, what's happening?"

"Oh thank you. I think I'm safer on dry land."

"Phew, it's getting hot. I'll shelter for a while in this cave."

"Whoops!"

"Mmm, this is nice and soft. I'll just dry myself off."

"Oh, excuse me. I thought you were a powder puff."

"Now I'm stuck, with no one to rescue me."

Tiny Ted's Big Adventure • Peter Bowman

"Thank you. Country people are very kind."

"But how do I get down?"

"By whirligig, of course! Whee!"

"Oh dear. No more sun."

"I think it's time to go home."

"But which way?"

"Oh, help. I'm lost and it's dark and I'm very, very small."

50

Tiny Ted's Big Adventure • Peter Bowman

"There you are," said Mouse.
"I'm glad I've found you."

"So am I," said Tiny Ted.
"I've had a big adventure.
But really…"

"…there's no place like home."

THE END

Susie Jenkin-Pearce

ROSIE AND THE PAVEMENT BEARS

Rosie was very small, the smallest in her class. And being small was not always fun...especially when Ben and Billy were around.
Ben and Billy were BULLIES. They pushed Rosie when Mrs Partridge wasn't looking, they pulled her hair and stuck out their tongues. They teased her on the way home.

"I shouldn't tread on the cracks if I were you!" jeered Billy.

"Nah!" sneered Ben. "The bears'll get you."

"Don't care," sniffed Rosie. "I'm not scared." And she stepped on the cracks on purpose. I wish the bears *would* come, thought Rosie. They can't be worse than Billy and Ben. So...

Rosie stepped on the cracks on the way to school. She stepped on the cracks all the way home.

She stepped on the cracks on the way to the park. AND... not one bear, not a paw, not a whisker.

Then one morning, as Rosie walked to school, the thought of those big bullies was more than she could stand.

Rosie and the Pavement Bears • Susie Jenkin-Pearce

"It's not FAIR!" she shouted. "Why don't they leave me alone?" and she stamped her foot down so hard that she bit her tongue and burst into tears.

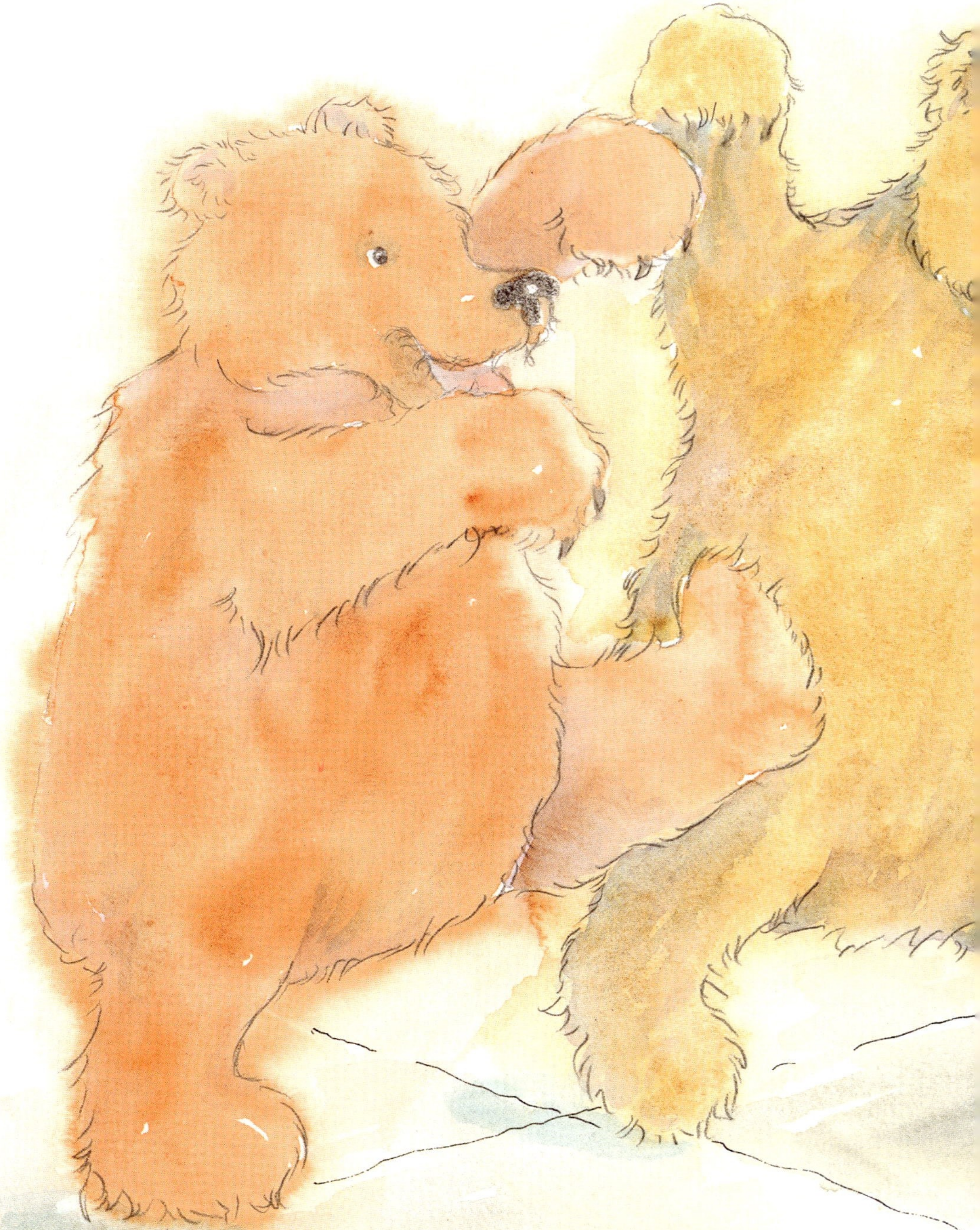

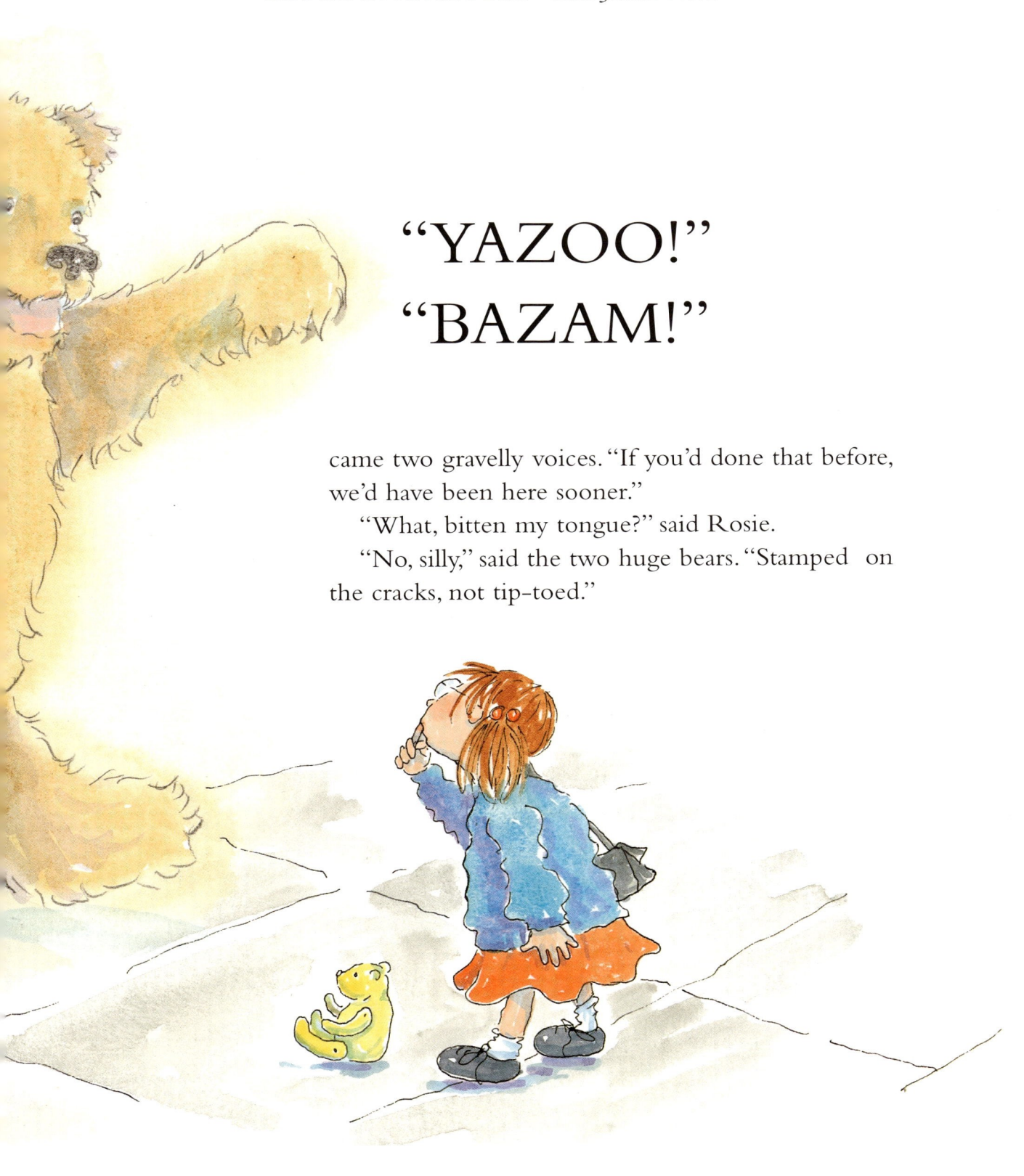

Rosie and the Pavement Bears • Susie Jenkin-Pearce

"YAZOO!"
"BAZAM!"

came two gravelly voices. "If you'd done that before, we'd have been here sooner."

"What, bitten my tongue?" said Rosie.

"No, silly," said the two huge bears. "Stamped on the cracks, not tip-toed."

Rosie felt good as she marched through the school gates. With two big bears beside her, she'd have no problems.

In class, Rosie knew all the answers.

For sums, she had her fingers *and* two sets of paws to count on.

In writing, her work looked much neater when *she* wasn't being pushed.

Rosie and the Pavement Bears • Susie Jenkin-Pearce

In PE she jumped higher than anyone in the class ever had before. Ben and Billy didn't do too well at all.

Then at lunchtime, the two bullies did some extremely silly things. Mr Robin was very cross. Suddenly Ben and Billy seemed rather stupid.

At storytime Rosie amazed everyone by telling the best bear stories they had ever heard. She had lots of great ideas.

Going home, Rosie felt happier than she had ever felt before.

But as she rounded the corner of her street, she was horrified to see two big girls blocking the way of a small boy.

Rosie bristled with anger.

"Go on, Rosie," said the bears. "Get 'em!"

Rosie and the Pavement Bears • Susie Jenkin-Pearce

Rosie took a deep breath.
"How DARE you!" she roared.
"Pick on someone your own size."

The two big girls looked at Rosie in surprise. Suddenly they were afraid. She had the look of an angry bear.

Rosie took the little boy's hand.

"No need to be afraid," said Rosie. "Not with the Pavement Bears to help us."

But when she looked round, the Pavement Bears had gone.

"Yazoo! Bazam!" sang Rosie, and they jumped on the cracks all the way home.

Benedict Blathwayt
BEAR IN THE AIR

It was time to go out. Lucy was going shopping with Mum. She put Bear in the shopping basket with some letters that had to be posted.

When they walked through the park, Bear could hear music playing in the distance. As they went further down the path, the music got louder and louder. Bear was excited. What could it be?

Bear in the Air • Benedict Blathwayt

It was a fair!

Bear had never ridden a horse before. Round and round they went on the carousel; up and down went the colourful horses. Bear wanted another go, but Lucy had seen the rockets. "Come on, Bear!" she cried.

Lucy held on to Bear tightly as the rocket flew higher and higher. Bear waved at the people down below.

Next they tried the big wheel. Up and up and UP! Faster and faster and faster. Bear wanted to go even higher, but the wheel began to slow down and suddenly they were back to earth again.

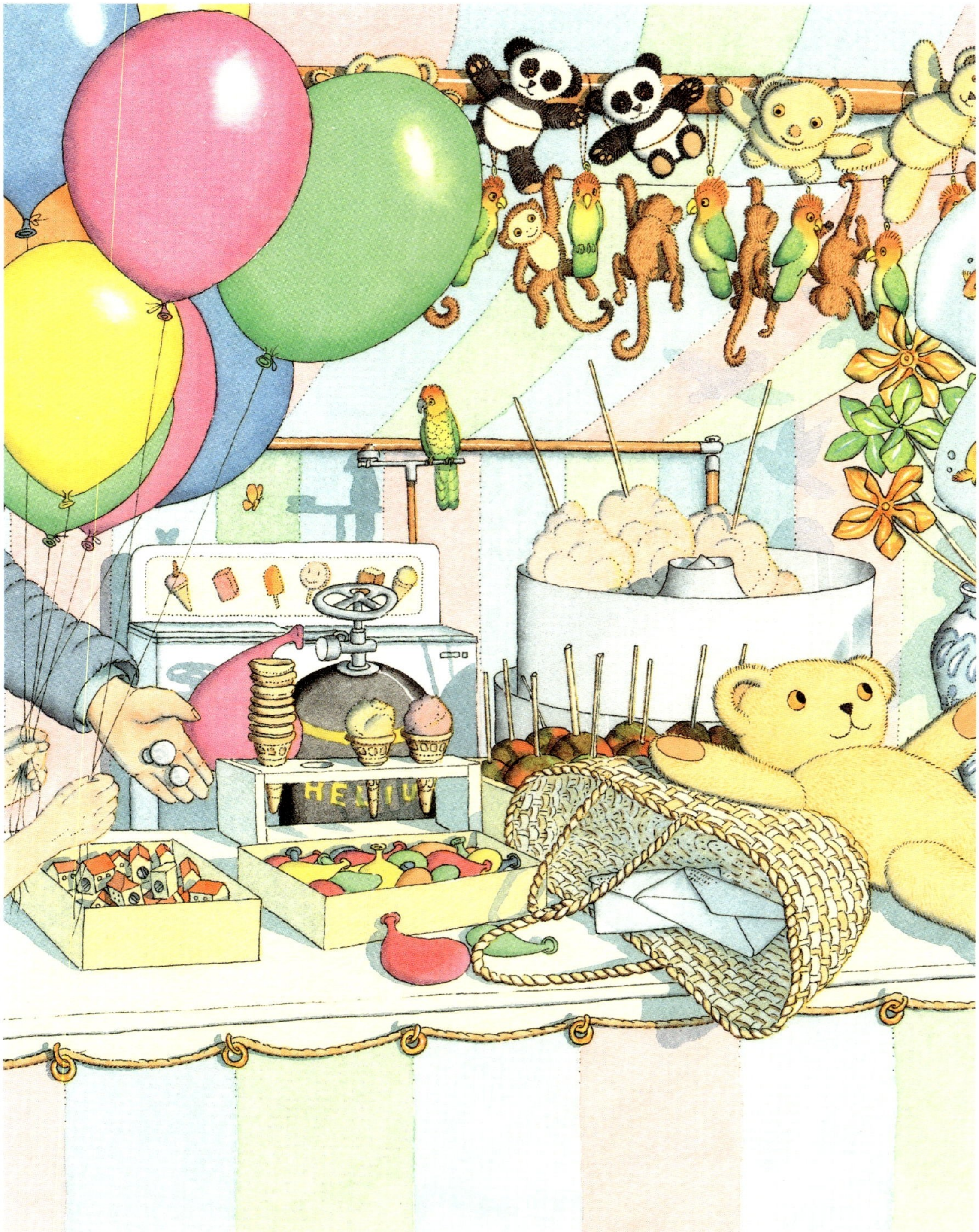

Bear in the Air • Benedict Blathwayt

Lucy's mum gave her money to buy some balloons. Lucy tied them to the basket to stop them blowing away.

Suddenly there was a gust of wind. Oh, no! The basket and Bear were lifted into the air. "Come back!" cried Lucy. But it was too late.

This is high, thought Bear. This is *very* high. But still he drifted up and up. This is TOO high.

He flew into the evening…

Bear in the Air • Benedict Blathwayt

through the night…

and into the next day.

Lucy will be missing me, thought Bear sadly. Will I ever land?

It began to rain.

Bear and the basket became very wet and heavy. Down they sank, with a BANG and a BUMP! An old lady found Bear in a vegetable patch. His address was found on the back of the letters.

He was sent home in a parcel. Lucy was overjoyed to see him again.
 "I thought I'd lost you," she said.
 Bear was very glad to be home. That's enough flying for me, he thought.

Caroline Castle

GRANDPA BODLEY AND THE PHOTOGRAPHS

Illustrated by Peter Bowman

ONE DAY GRANDPA BODLEY AND HUTCHINSON were clearing out the cupboard under the stairs when they came across a rusty old tin.
"I wonder what's inside?" said Hutchinson.
"Let's open it," said Grandpa, "then we'll find out."
Grandpa held firmly on to the back of the tin while Hutchinson pulled

at the lid. It snapped open with a ping.

A ghostly bear loomed out at them from the dark box.

"Ahhhhh!" screeched Hutchinson, jumping back in fright.

"Silly," laughed Grandpa. "It's only a photograph."

Hutchinson and Grandpa Bodley looked at the photograph. The big teddy face seemed to be staring straight at them. Bodley put on his glasses and studied it carefully. There was something familiar about this strange bear. "Yes, yes," he said. "Those ears, that nose, that particular way of smiling…it's your Great-grandad Dutton when he was a young bear. It's a self-portrait."

Bodley turned the tin upside down. A great shower of photographs flew out and soon there were bears all over the floor. "Do you know something," said Grandpa in a whisper, "I do believe we've found Great-grandad Dutton's famous photograph collection."

With mounting excitement the two bears collected the photographs and carried them to the kitchen table.

"Well, what did I say?" said Grandpa Bodley, picking up the first one. "Here he is again, on his wedding day."

Hutchinson saw a very smart bear dressed in a funny long coat with a flower in the buttonhole. "When was that?" he asked.

"Oh, years and years ago," said Bodley. "Before he got all crinkly and lost his fur."

Grandpa Bodley and the Photographs • Caroline Castle & Peter Bowman

Hutchinson pulled another one from the middle of the pile. It was of a small bear in a smart school uniform looking very prim and stiff.

"Why, that's me!" exclaimed Grandpa Bodley, "on my first day at big school. I was scared half to death. They were very strict in those days, so you had to watch out."

"You don't look very comfortable," said Hutchinson.

Grandpa laughed. "I wasn't," he said, rubbing his neck. "I hated my school uniform. I can still feel that scratchy collar to this day."

"Who's this teddy?" asked Hutchinson, picking up another photograph. It was a fuzzy snapshot of a pretty young bear reading a book.

"Oh, goodness me," said Grandpa. "It's Grandma Bodley when I first met her. I gave her that book for her birthday."

"Where's Grandma Bodley now?" asked Hutchinson. "Why isn't she here?"

Grandpa's eyes misted over. "Ahem," he said. "There's a thing." For a moment he looked very sad. Then he smiled and sniffed into his hanky. "I think I've got a cold coming on," he said.

The next photograph was a bit blurry. Hutchinson held it up to the window. Grandpa took a deep breath. "The coronation of Queen Elizabear the Second," he said importantly. "I drove the whole family to London in my new motorcar. We all dressed up for the occasion. Great-grandad was getting on a bit by then and needed a walking stick."

It really was a beautiful picture, with the young

queen waving to the crowd from a golden carriage. "Hey," said Hutchinson, "she looks as if she's waving straight at Grandma Bodley."

"I wouldn't be surprised if she was," laughed Grandpa. "Grandma fought her way to the front and nearly wore herself out cheering and waving."

Grandpa was beginning to get a little hungry. "Time we had a break," he said. "Why, it's nearly lunchtime."

Grandpa Bodley made some tea and Hutchinson helped with the sandwiches.

"Oh, happy memories," sighed Grandpa, thinking fondly of Grandma Bodley.

Hutchinson gobbled down his sandwich as fast as he could. "I'm ready for more photos now," he said.

"Hold your horses," laughed Grandpa. "You can't rush a good cup of tea."

After lunch Grandpa put his glasses back on and the two bears, the big old one and the very little young one, settled down to look at the rest of the photographs.

"Well I never," said Grandpa. "Here's our old house at Buttonear Road. And look, who do you think that is on the bicycle?"

Hutchinson looked hard. It was a small girl bear about four years old.

"I'll tell you who it is," said Grandpa Bodley. "It's your mum when she was a little bear. We bought her that bicycle for her birthday. She was very wobbly at first but she soon learned to ride. She was determined not to be afraid."

Hutchinson loved the photograph. He had never thought of his mum as a little bear.

"Now here we are," said Grandpa, picking up a photograph that had fallen on the floor. "The great Oxford and Cambridge bear race. We took a picnic. There's your mum again and Grandma Bodley holding the flowers, and that's me with the glasses."

"Look!" said Hutchinson, pointing to a small bear in a red jacket. "He's taking the last piece of cake while no one's looking."

"Aha," said Bodley. "It's my dreadful nephew Hamish. He was spoilt to death, and greedy with it. You know, I always wondered how that cake disappeared so quickly!"

Grandpa lay down on the sofa to stretch his legs.

"Look at this," said Hutchinson. "A Christmas one."

Grandpa adjusted his glasses, peered closely, then laughed and laughed. It was Christmas time and the whole family was gathered round the tree. "I remember this as if it were yesterday," he said. "There's Aunt Hamilton and my horrible nephew Hamish again. That photograph was taken just after he'd put a piece of holly on Great-grandma Dutton's chair as she was sitting down. If you look closely you'll see that he's crying."

"What happened?" said Hutchinson.

"He got a smack, that's what," said Grandpa. "And about time too. He'd been so naughty, it's a wonder Father Christmas came at all."

Hutchinson pounced on the next photograph with a shriek.

"I know who these are!" he cried. "It's my mum and dad."

"That's right," said Bodley. "It was taken just before their wedding. They were so much in love that they hardly noticed anyone else. Great-grandad Dutton was very old by then. Ninety-seven at least. He died the next year. Dear old thing."

Hutchinson felt rather sad. "But at least he left these photographs," he said. "To remember him by."

Grandpa Bodley and the Photographs • Caroline Castle & Peter Bowman

They were nearing the end of the pile. Grandpa didn't say but Hutchinson could tell he was getting tired. He always rubbed his eyes when he felt sleepy.

They had come to the last photograph. Grandpa picked it up carefully. It was of a very, very small bear all bristly and new and wrapped up in a blue blanket.

"Who's that?" asked Hutchinson.

"Why, that's *you*, young teddy," whispered Grandpa. "Just after you were born." He walked over to his chair, leaned heavily back and pulled Hutchinson on to his knee. Hutchinson touched the old bear's cheek.

"Why are you crying, Grandpa?" he asked.

"Oh, I don't know," sighed Grandpa. "I must be getting old."

And Hutchinson sat warm and tight on Grandpa's lap until the sun went down and the old bear was asleep.

John Richardson
BAD MOOD BEAR

"Good night," said Mum.
"Good night," said Dad.

But Bear didn't go to sleep.

First he played with his soldiers, then he read his picture book, and then he tiptoed out on to the landing to listen to the noise of the television.

Soon he began to feel thirsty. He went downstairs to ask for a glass of water.

"You'll be tired tomorrow," warned Dad.

At breakfast next morning, Bear threw his porridge on the floor.

"Goodness me!" said Grandma Bear.
"Good heavens!" said Mum and Dad together.
But Bear just growled. "I'm in a bad mood," he said.

Mum gathered Bad Mood Bear up in her arms and took him out into the garden.

She put him on the swing to cheer him up.

But Bear had a tantrum. He fell over backwards and bumped his head.

"Stupid swing," said Bear, bursting into tears.

"Let me rub your bump better," said Mum.

"Leave me alone, you!" screamed Bear.

So, Mum did.

As soon as Mum was gone, he picked up a big stick and hit the swing as hard as he could.

What a bad mood bear!

Bear could see Grandma and Grandad watching him from the window.

He poked his tongue out at them.
"That bear needs a good smack," said Grandad.
Grandma agreed.

"Hello, Bear," said the pigs from next door. "This is our new friend, Goat."
"So what!" snarled Bear.

"We're going down to the river to play, are you coming?"
"No, you don't play properly," replied Bear rudely.

Goat said that Bear wasn't very nice and they were better off without him.

"He's not *our* friend any more," said Pig.

Bear mooched around, kicking stones and growling. A fly buzzed around his nose.

"Buzz off!" screamed Bear, flapping his arms around in a temper.

Grandad was gardening in the vegetable patch and laughed to see Bear jumping around in such a rage.

"Bad Mood Bear, calm down and stop making such a fuss!" he called out.

And do you know what Bear did?!

That bad mood bear ran over and kicked Grandad's leg!

"Ouch!" shouted Grandad as he fell over.

Dad rushed out angrily. He grabbed Bear by the ear, took him up to his bedroom and smacked his bottom.

"We've had enough of your bad mood," he said. "Behave yourself!"

Bad Mood Bear screamed and screamed.

He screamed so hard that his throat hurt and his eyes ran.

Then he pulled a few rude faces, but it wasn't much fun when there was no one there to see them.

92

Bad Mood Bear • John Richardson

Later on, Mum brought Bad Mood Bear a glass of milk and a biscuit.
Outside a bee was humming in a sleepy sort of way.

Bad Mood Bear yawned; very soon he began to feel tired.
Mum closed the curtains. Within seconds Bad Mood Bear was asleep.

Bear slept for a long, long time.
When he woke up he smiled his first smile of the day.

At lunch time when Mum gave Bear his fish fingers he said, "Thank you," very politely, and ate them all up.

After he had licked the bowl clean he thought about all the naughty things he had done that morning.

"I'm sorry I was a bad mood bear," he said.

Later on Bear joined his friends at the river. "Can I play too?" he asked.

"Only if you promise not to be in a bad mood," said Pig.

"I promise," said Bear.

And he was a good mood bear all afternoon.

Shirley Isherwood

SOMETHING NEW FOR A BEAR TO DO

Illustrated by Reg Cartwright

ONE MORNING, Mr Manders woke with an interesting thought in his head. He woke the little bear, Edward James, to tell him about it. "It is this," said Mr Manders. "Why do bears always do the things that bears do? Why don't they do other things?"

Edward James said that he didn't know. He wanted to go back to sleep, but Mr Manders took him by the paw, and led him out into the garden, to discuss the matter further.

It was very early in the morning. The garden was full of mist and the birds were waking up and singing in the branches of the trees.

"That is what I mean," said Mr Manders. "Why do birds sing so beautifully in the trees, and bears don't?"

He climbed a tree, sat down on a branch and began to sing. His voice was very deep and low. "OO-ROO-OO-ROW," he sang – then he looked down at Edward James. "How do I sound?" he asked.

"Like a bear singing in a tree," said Edward James.

Mr Manders sighed. He came down from the tree, and together he and Edward James went on through the garden, to where a little stream ran over the stones and pebbles. As they drew near, a frog jumped from the grass and into the water.

"Now that is something that bears don't often do," said Mr Manders – and straight away he took a deep breath, flung himself forward, and sat down in the water. Then he sighed and climbed out again.

"And the reason they don't," he said as he sat by Edward James' side, "is, it isn't very interesting."

He lay down, and after a time the sun came out, his fur began to dry, and a little cloud of steam rose from his wet tummy.

As Mr Manders lay there gently steaming, a party of ants came by – each ant carrying a scrap of straw or a tiny ball of earth. "Now that is interesting," said Mr Manders. "They are working – building – and a bear could do that!"

He got up, and as Edward James watched, he began to collect stones and twigs. He picked them up and carried them across the garden, and put them down – just as the ants had done. Very soon he had built a little heap of stones and twigs, and he stood there gazing at it.

"What is it?" asked Edward James.

"It's plain to see what it is," said Mr Manders. "It's a sort of…well, I'm not sure what it is," he said, as he and Edward James climbed through the gap in the fence, "but it must be something."

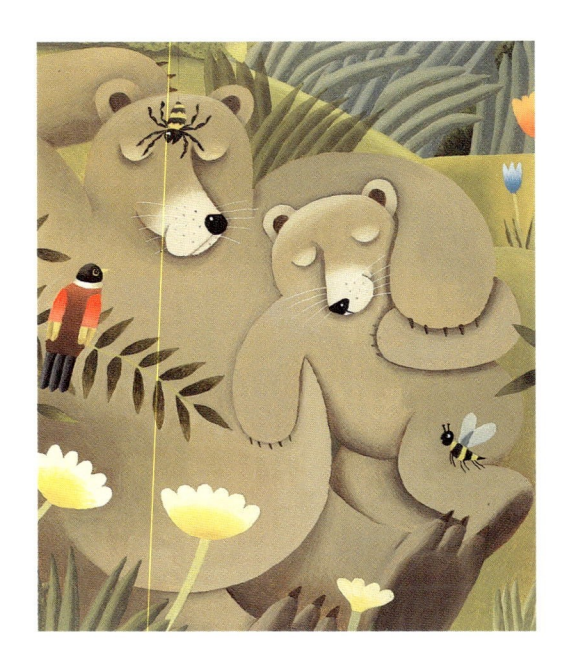

They crossed the field, lay down under the hedge and very soon fell asleep.

When Mr Manders awoke he found a spider dangling over his face on the end of a long fine thread. As Mr Manders watched, the spider ran up and down the thread, like a little yo-yo on the end of a piece of string.

'Now that is a nice new thing for a bear to do,' said Mr Manders, and he searched beneath the hedge until he found an old piece of string.

"I shall go up and down," he said, as he climbed a tree and tied the end of the string to a branch. Then he tied the other end of the string round his tummy, and jumped.

"Or not," he said, as he hung in the air above Edward James' head.

Something New for a Bear to Do • Shirley Isherwood & Reg Cartwright

He began to scrabble about wildly, but this only made him spin round and round.

"You see, Edward James," he said, when at last he stopped spinning, "one needs a lot of legs to go up and down, and I've only got two."

The string broke and he fell into the soft grass.

"I can't seem to do anything new at all," he said.

But as he lay, he heard someone moving in the earth. The next moment, Mole popped out.

"Excuse me," he said, "I meant to dig to the right, and instead I've dug to the left!" He came out of the hole, turned himself round and went back the way he had come.

"That seems an interesting thing to do, Edward James," said Mr Manders, "and it is what I shall do." He began to dig, and Edward James sat and wondered if Mr Manders meant to live in a hole, like Mole, and if he, Edward James, would have to live in

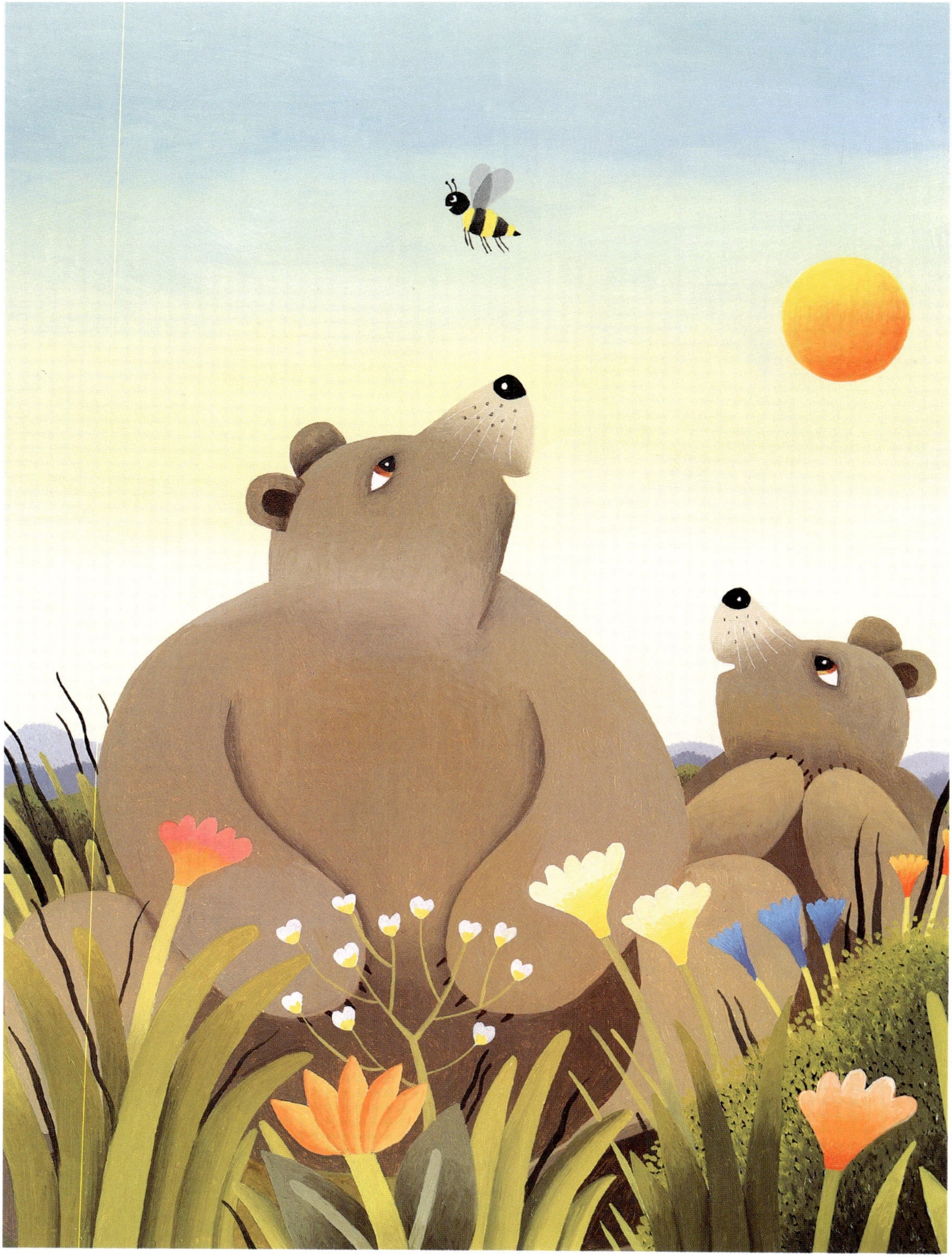

the hole as well. He hoped not, for he liked the house where he and Mr Manders lived. He liked the kitchen with its bright fire, and he liked his bedroom with his own little bed.

As he stood and wondered, Mr Manders scrabbled out. He was covered in earth, and he blinked in the bright sunlight. "Moles dig holes," he said, "but I don't think bears care for them much."

He gazed at Edward James sadly. "What new thing *can* I do?" he said.

"Just be a bear," said Edward James.

As he spoke a nice fat bee flew by.

"What a good idea, Edward James!" said Mr Manders. "I could get lots of honey for our tea!" and he got up and trotted off to the house. When he came out he had brushed the earth from his fur and was wearing his yellow and black striped sweater.

"How do I look, Edward James?" he said.

"Like a bear in a yellow and black striped sweater," said Edward James, but softly to himself, for Mr Manders was already making his way down to the bottom of the garden, where the beehives stood. He was gone for such a long time that at last Edward James went to look for him.

He found Mr Manders sitting in the long grass, gazing sadly at the beehives. "It's a question of bears being large, Edward James," he said, "and bees being small, and beehive doors being small, and the honey being inside. If you understand what I mean."

Edward James said that he thought he understood. He helped Mr Manders to his feet, and together they went for a walk round the field.

As they went, Mr Manders thought of all the things he'd tried to be. "A singing bird, an ant, a frog, a spider, a mole and a bee," he said, "and really, I'm just a foolish old bear."

"No you're not!" said Edward James. "You're a bear with imagination, a bear with ambition, a bear with ideas, and I like you just the way you are." Mr Manders was so pleased to hear Edward James say this that he gave him a big hug. It was a lovely warm hug, and it made Edward James feel safe and happy.

Mr Manders felt happy too, and gave a deep low growl. It was a wonderful sound, and everyone who lived in the field said, "Oh, what a wonderful growl he has!" - except for some very new fieldmice, who thought that the growl might be thunder and hurried home before the rain began to fall.

Something New for a Bear to Do · Shirley Isherwood & Reg Cartwright

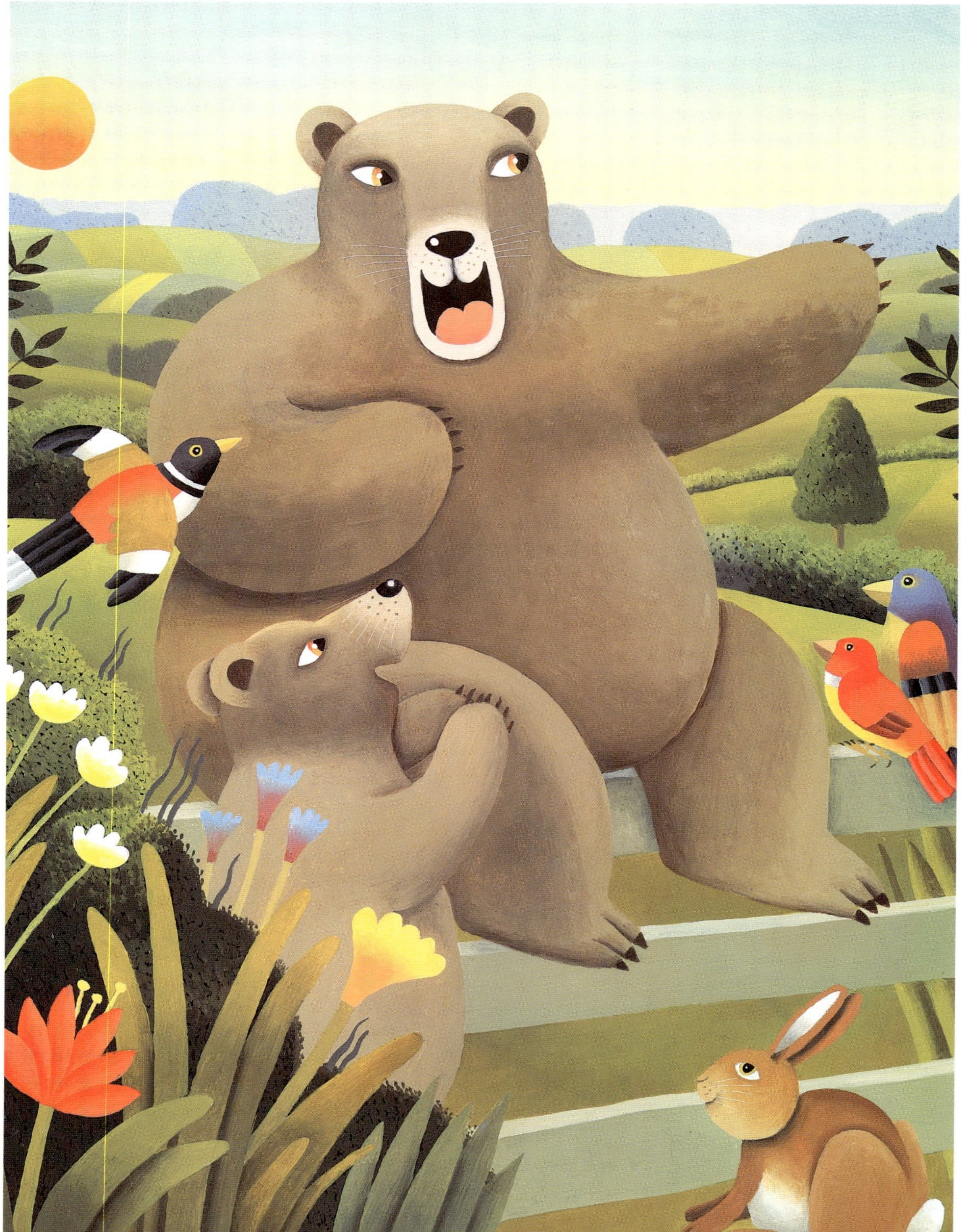

Something New for a Bear to Do • Shirley Isherwood & Reg Cartwright

Mr Manders and Edward James began to make their way home. But before they went through the gap in the hedge, Mr Manders climbed up on to the fence, sat down, and began to sing. "OO-ROO-OO-ROW!" he sang.

"How did I sound?" he asked when the song was ended.

"Like a bear singing on a fence," said Edward James. "A bear singing *beautifully* on a fence," he added – and with that they both went in for tea.

Alison Sage
TEDDYBEARS ON STAGE
Illustrated by Susanna Gretz

Today was the day of the play. Andrew kept saying his part over and over again.
"Is that the sun? Winter is done…"
"Shh!" said Sara. "They're coming!"
The audience came in.

"Do we get ice-creams now?" asked William.
"Shh!" said Great Uncle Jerome. "The curtain's about to go up…"

Louise was the Queen of Winter.
"*Brr! Brr!*" she said. "*Everything's freezing!
Our toes are cold and we can't stop sneezing!
It's winter time; we can't hear a sound
Because there's a blanket of snow on the ground.*"

"Stop pushing me," said Andrew. "You didn't push Louise."
"*She's* saying her lines right," said Sara.

Louise droned on,
"The snow has gone; the farmer needs
To work his hardest and plant
the seeds…"

"You're late!" hissed Louise,
as Andrew scattered
the seeds.

Then Louise beamed at the audience.
"Down comes the rain; the winds are blowing;
But deep in the ground, our seeds are growing.
Down comes the rain!" she said, a bit louder.

Teddybears on Stage • Susanna Gretz & Alison Sage

At last it rained.

"Now the wind!" said Sara.
Robert rustled the curtain.
"And mind that *hose*, Andrew..."

Suddenly, there was a terrific storm.

Teddybears on Stage • Susanna Gretz & Alison Sage

"Curtain!" shrieked Sara, and the curtain fell.

"Now is it time for ice-creams?" asked William. "Time?" said Great Uncle Jerome. "Yes, I *am* having a good time. And they seem to be, too, don't they?"

But backstage, they were *not* having a good time.
"Stop it!" cried Sara. "We've got to start the second half."

"That's *my* hat!" said Louise.
"Well, I can't find mine,
and I'm on next!"
said Andrew.
"Curtain's going up!"
yelled Sara.

Andrew looked at the audience. There was silence; *what* was he supposed to say? Slowly Andrew moved one arm. I look like a teapot, he thought.

"I *am a* little teapot,"
he sang softly,
"short and stout..."
"He's not supposed
to sing anything,"
said Louise.
The audience began to smile.
"He's spoiling everything,"
said Louise.

But Andrew began again.
"I'm a little teapot, short and stout,
Here is my handle, here is my spout,
When I get all steamed up, then I shout – "

"Bravo!"

"TIP ME OVER
AND POUR ME OUT!"

"Huh," said Louise. "What a flop."
But everyone else cheered.

"Why won't Andrew take off his make-up?" asked Robert, as they went home.

"Because he's the *star*," said William.

Suzy-Jane Tanner
WATCH OUT FOR FRED!

Ursulina and Frederika Brown are twins. They start the day looking just the same. They're never the same for long, though.

Fred always seems to get covered in whatever she is doing.

Like the time they were painting a picture for Mum.

"Watch out for Fred!" warned Dad.

As usual it was too late. Fred sat in the paintbox anyway.

Then there was the time Ursulina put on a ballet show with her friends.

Ursulina was Sleeping Beauty.

Fred *started out* as a sugar plum fairy.

But as usual she ended up as a monster.

"Watch out for Fred!" said Ursulina.

The monster tripped over Sleeping Beauty on her way to ride her bike instead.

Watch Out for Fred! • *Suzy-Jane Tanner*

One morning the phone rang.

"It's Cousin Grizelda," said Mum. "She wants you to be bridesmaids at her wedding."

"Goody!" cried Ursulina.

"Ugh!" gasped Fred.

"They'd be delighted," announced Mum into the phone.

Mum took the twins to Bruin's Bridal Boutique to hire the bridesmaids' dresses.

The dresses were pink and frilly.

"Don't they look sweet!" cooed the saleslady.

"Yuk!" said Fred.

"Watch out for Fred!" said Mum, as Fred chose a topper from the bottom of the pile.
"I hate pink!" muttered Fred.

The morning of the wedding arrived. Mum washed Ursulina's fur first.
"Watch out for Fred!" called Mum, as Fred tried to escape.
Dad caught her just in time.
Fred hated having her fur washed.

Mum helped the twins put on their bridesmaids' dresses.
Ursulina sat nice and still.
"But it itches!" grumbled Fred.

Watch Out for Fred! • Suzy-Jane Tanner

Then it was Mum's turn. She sat Ursulina and Fred on the bed so she could keep an eye on them. Mum put on her prettiest dress. She had a new hat too.

"Watch out for Fred!" reminded Dad, as Fred reached out to help Mum powder her nose.

At last everyone was ready to leave. On the way to the car, Fred spotted an interesting-looking worm.

"Watch out for Fred!" yelled Dad. "It's still muddy from last night's rain."

Mum and Dad marched either side of Fred down the path to the car.

They parked down the road from the church. Fred wondered whether the engine oil needed checking.

"Watch out for Fred!" sighed Mum.

She stuck close to Fred all the way to the church.

Watch Out for Fred! • Suzy-Jane Tanner

The Browns waited by the door for Cousin Grizelda.
　　Family and friends had come from all over the world to be at the wedding.

Ursulina kissed Grandma nicely.
　　Fred didn't want to be kissed at all. She wriggled and squirmed, and got lipstick all over her face. Fred was cleaned up just as Cousin Grizelda arrived.

After the wedding, it was time for the photographs.

"Smile please!" said the photographer.

"Watch out for Fred!" warned Dad, as Fred pulled her best monster face instead.

Dad took Fred to stand right at the back.

There was a photograph of Cousin Grizelda throwing her bouquet in the air. Ursulina caught it.

Watch Out for Fred! • *Suzy-Jane Tanner*

Then everyone lined up for a photograph together.
Ursulina stood right at the front with the bouquet. She decided to do some ballet on her own.

Ursulina was so carried away with her pirouettes that she didn't notice the big muddy puddle.
"Watch out for...

...Ursulina!"

Watch Out for Fred! • *Suzy-Jane Tanner*

SNAP went the camera.

It was Fred's favourite photograph. They even printed it in the local paper. Fred decided it wasn't so bad being a bridesmaid after all.

"Now I suppose we'll have to watch out for Fred *and* Ursulina!" sighed Mum.